# Everyone Has a Story to Tell

Tips & Activities for Emerging Writers

**Zetta Elliott**

Rosetta
&
Press

ISBN-10: 1987455657
ISBN-13: 978-1987455656

for dreamers everywhere

# Everyone Has a Story to Tell

# Table of Contents

# Let's Write!

Everyone has a story to tell! I put those words above the board in my Freedom School classroom in Bed-Stuy, Brooklyn back in 1998, and it has since become my mantra. I think of myself as an educator, but I am not a teacher. I'm not certified or licensed, and my doctoral degree is in American Studies, not Education. But I was raised by two public school teachers, and I've worked with kids for close to thirty years. I've published just as many books for young readers, and every year I conduct dozens of writing workshops in schools, libraries, and on college campuses. So I guess that makes me qualified to write this guide!

I met Erin Miller, a professor of Reading and Elementary Education at UNC Charlotte, at the annual NCTE conference in 2016. She and her colleagues invited me to their campus, and Erin explained that most textbooks available to her featured novels and picture books that don't reflect the diverse students her pre-service teachers are likely to encounter in their classrooms. This isn't a textbook; it's just a collection of activities that I use when I'm working with kids, teens, and adults. I hope that by sharing some of my own teaching tools I can support those educators who are committed to creating an inclusive learning environment.

Teachers often reach out to me asking for lesson plans to accompany my books, and I regret having to turn them away. I know that many "classics" are taught over and over largely because there are so many resources available to teachers who don't always have the time to develop new curriculum materials for recently released novels. Most of the activities in this guide are based on my own books, but I think they're easily transferable to other texts you may be using in your classroom. When I visit schools, I often have just one class period--less than an hour--to conduct a writing workshop. The prompts I use are designed to get students writing quickly, but these lessons can be expanded as needed.

Everyone has a story to tell. I grew up in Canada struggling to see myself in the books I read in school. The stories I write today are part of my healing process, and I don't want any child to experience the same shameful invisibility. If you can't find books that accurately reflect the students in your school, don't wait on the publishing industry—make your own books! This guide concludes with some resources to help you empower your students to become producers and not just consumers of books.

I plan to publish many more books in the coming years, and so this guide may expand over time. For now, I hope these activities will inspire you to elevate and celebrate the voices of our youth!

# Warm-Ups

I've been writing seriously since I was thirteen, and at this point can easily sit down and start to type or write without any prompts. But most students I work with, regardless of their age, respond better to prompts when they've had a chance to warm up. Some writers find their imagination is activated by physical movement, and others find their fears are allayed by a simple activity that builds confidence. These three warm-ups are easily modified to suit any topic or text.

## Word Association

Get your students thinking associatively with word association. This fun, fast activity is a great conversation starter and provides you with crowd-sourced vocabulary words you can use for subsequent writing.

✓ Materials:
☐ pens or pencils
☐ paper
☐ timer

1.  Ask students to write the numbers one to ten down the margin of their paper.

2.  Explain that you will write one word on the board and give them one minute to write down all the words that pop into their head. Remind students that the goal is to write as many words as possible; urge them not to censor themselves or worry about spelling.

3.  Give them a demonstration: "If I said 'school,' what words immediately come to mind?" Allow students to share their words and remind them that they can list material objects (books, desks, pens), favorite subjects (math, gym, art) as well as words that describe how they feel (bored, stressed, empowered).

4.  Make sure students understand the activity. "You have one minute to write down as many words as you can that you associate with…" Write the word on the board and/or say it aloud. Start your timer.

5.  Guide students if they seem to be struggling. When I lead workshops on my picture book BIRD, I use the word "bird" for a warm-up. After about 15 seconds have gone by, I start to give them prompts: "What do birds eat? Where do they live? Which sports teams are named after birds? Which birds do WE eat? A bird is a symbol of…"

6.  Let students know when they have ten seconds left. When time's up, ask them to put down their pens and pencils. Ask how many students wrote down ten or more words. I often start with those students, asking them to give me three of their

words, which I write on the board. Other students must scratch off their own list words that have already been shared.

Word association is a quick, fun way for students to forge and share connections around a central topic or theme.

## Conversation Cards

I developed this activity for adults when I was writer-in-residence at Weeksville Heritage Center. I was teaching classes around the theme of home, community, and belonging. When we hosted a salon in one of the historic houses, I thought of the photographs genteel folks used to exchange and/or collect in the nineteenth century (cartes de visite). These conversation cards are somewhat different, but they're a great way to get kids, teens, and adults sharing, connecting, and moving around.

✓ Materials:
☐ colored construction paper or cardstock

☐ timer

1. Come up with several questions that relate to the book under consideration.

2. Print them onto cardstock.

3. Distribute the cards to everyone who will participate.

4. Have students stand up and find a partner. It helps if you can clear a space in the room so people can move around easily.

5. Explain that the students will have one minute to answer their partner's question. You can give more time if the questions are complex, but the goal is to keep people moving.

6. Set the timer. When the allotted time is up, ask students to swap cards and find a new partner. Set the timer once more and start again.

You can call out "Swap!" as many times as you like, and it's fine if questions repeat since new responses can be given or the same response can be given to a different questioner.

Here are some of the questions I developed for my salon at the historic house. I adapted some of these and used them for a younger audience:

- Name one thing about your home or community that helps you thrive.
- I know I belong in a place when I feel...
- Name two things that weaken a home.
- When you're away from home, what do you miss most?
- The happiest homes have these three things: _____, _____, _____.

- Name one thing you feel would strengthen your community?
- What will your community look like in ten years?
- What lesson did you learn at home that has best served you over the years?
- Describe your happiest memory of your childhood home.
- What would make your ancestors proud if they could see your community today?

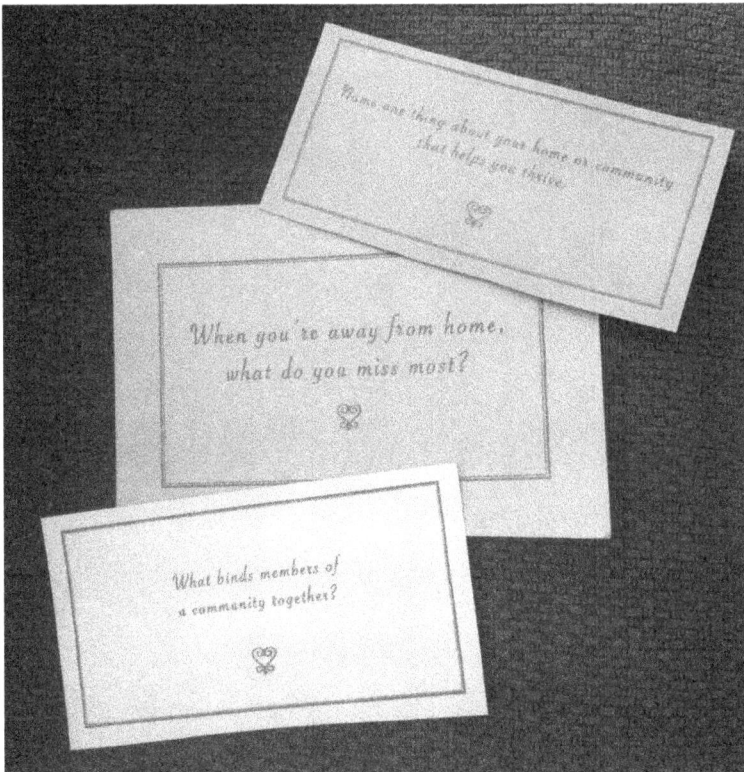

# Précis Strips

I developed this activity for students who were studying BIRD. When I was in high school, we regularly were asked to read an essay or short story and then develop a précis statement or concise summary. Instead of a statement, for this warm-up activity I ask students to consider the essential events in a story. This can be especially challenging for lengthy novels or films, which can include many subplots and characters (just try asking students to list the ten most important scenes in *Black Panther*). This warm-up requires students to work collaboratively, which helps if some students struggle with comprehension or simply haven't finished reading the book. If the book is available, students can consult it during the activity to verify their results.

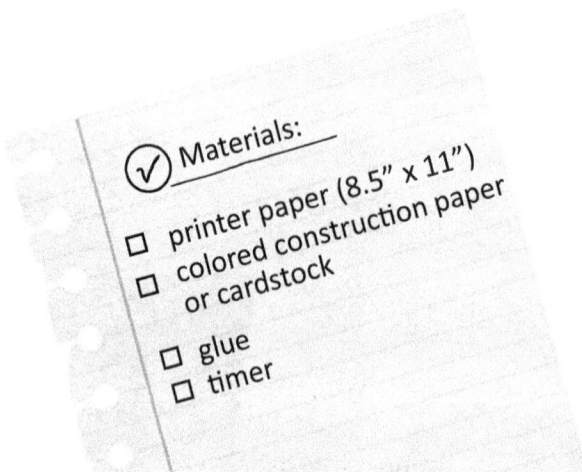

(✓) Materials:

☐ printer paper (8.5" x 11")
☐ colored construction paper or cardstock

☐ glue
☐ timer

1. Make a chronological list of events that transpire in the book. Type (or write down) the ten most important ones.

2. Print the sheet with your listed events (I recommend double- or triple-spacing). Cut out each event so that you have ten strips. Glue each one to a rectangular piece of colored construction paper or cardstock. You will need a set of ten strips for each group of students.

1. Shuffle the strips and bind each set with a large paper clip.

2. Put students into groups of three or four. Give each group of bundle of strips and tell them to spread them out on the desk—face down.

3. Explain the activity. You can give them a set amount of time or offer a small reward for the first team to arrange the strips in the correct order. Urge students to read all the strips first and to consult the book if they're unsure about the sequence of events.

4. Print a master list for yourself so that you can circulate and offer suggestions or hints. When time is up or all teams think they're done, allow students to read out their sequence and correct or challenge one another. Ask students to describe scenes in greater details and/or to guess at the author's intent in having the plot unfold this way.

5. Ask each group to bind their ten strips before turning them in. Remember to shuffle the strips prior to using them again.

Bird loves going to the park to feed the birds with Uncle Son.

Bird likes to draw, and learns about art from his brother, Marcus.

Marcus doesn't go to school and goes up on the roof to use drugs.

Uncle Son shares a lesson with Bird, who now understands that Marcus is at peace.

While the family is at church, Marcus steals their valuables.

Below are the ten-point summaries I developed for three of my books.

## Précis Strips for BIRD

1. Bird likes to draw the things he sees in his world.

2. Bird loves going to the park to feed the birds with Uncle Son.

3. Bird likes to draw, and learns about art from his brother Marcus.

4. Marcus doesn't go to school and goes up on the roof to use drugs.

5. Marcus starts to change and looks sick.

6. While the family is at church, Marcus steals their valuables.

7. Though he's not allowed inside, Marcus comes by to give Bird a gift.

8. Bird wishes he could fix Marcus, but he can't and Marcus dies.

9. Grandad dies, too, and now Uncle Son takes Bird to the park so they can name all the birds.

10. Uncle Son shares a lesson with Bird, who now understands that Marcus is at peace.

## Précis Strips for MELENA'S JUBILEE

1. Melena wakes up with a song in her heart.
2. A guest tripped over Melena's toys, banged into the table, and broke her mother's vase.
3. Melena discovers her family has forgiven her.
4. Melena decides not to hit her brother.
5. Melena finds food for lunch growing in her grandmother's garden.
6. Helen tells Melena to make Gavin to pay back the money he owes her.
7. Melena and her friends pool their money to buy a hot fudge sundae.
8. The friends go to the playground to eat.
9. The friends realize that sunshine is free.
10. Melena discovers that the song in her heart is about having a chance to start over every day!

## Précis Strips for SHIP OF SOULS

1. D tries to be perfect so that Mrs. Martin won't send him back to the group home.

2. Keem helps D when two bullies try to take his pizza.

3. Nyla invites D to sit with her at lunch.

4. D finds a wounded bird in the park and decides to take it home.

5. The nether beings set a trap for D in the park.

6. Nyla blackmails her stepmother into taking care of D.

7. Nuru sends a signal to raise the dead.

8. The nether beings create a stone beast that stabs Nyla in the park.

9. Billy, a young patriot, helps D escape from the root cage.

10. Nuru leads the four friends to the Chamber of Souls.

## Bird

Though it came out in 2008, BIRD remains one of my most popular books. The story of a family impacted by addiction was inspired by my older brother who served as the inspiration for the character Marcus. When I present on BIRD, I talk about how my brother's theft started with the microwave and escalated until he wound up in jail. I talk about how shame kept me silent for years but when I finally shared my story, I discovered I wasn't alone. Lots of families have been affected by traumatic events, and all kids have lost someone in their lives that they'd like to memorialize. This three-part workshop builds upon memories of a loved one, giving writers the opportunity to reflect on the legacy their loved one left behind.

### 1.

### Sankofa Postcards

(✓) Materials:
- ☐ pens or pencils
- ☐ paper
- ☐ timer
- ☐ cardstock
- ☐ "Postcards from Far Away" by Coldplay
- ☐ computer (or other music-playing device)

1.  Explain the word association warm-up activity; ask students to write the numbers one to ten down the margin of their sheet of paper.

2.  Set the timer and give students one minute to write down as many words as they can that they associate with "birds." Some students may need a prompt: Where do birds live? What do they eat? Which birds do WE eat? Which sports teams are named after birds?

3.  When time is up, ask students to put down their pens and share three of their words. If another student shares a word that's on their list, it must be crossed off to avoid repetition. You can write students' words on the board to create a word cloud.

4.  Ask students to define or give an example of a symbol. I sometimes use flashcards or slides that show a dove, the peace symbol, a dollar sign, and some adinkra symbols from the Akan people of West Africa (these are easily found online). I then show two adinkra symbols that represent the principle of SANKOFA. One symbol looks like a heart, and the other shows a bird looking back over its shoulder.

5.  Ask students to interpret the bird symbol. What's in its mouth? Why is it looking backward? Sankofa means "return to your source" or "go back and fetch it." I use the sankofa principle to guide my writing: "There is no shame in going back to retrieve something of value you left behind." When I wrote BIRD, I realized I had gone into my past to find something valuable—a lesson I could share with others. Then I no longer felt ashamed, and I was able to connect with other people who had had similar experiences.

Sankofa ~ "return to your source"
or "go back and fetch it"

6. Cue the track "Postcards from Far Away" by Coldplay. Explain to students that you will play this short song three times. Each time the song ends, you will ask them to write something down. Students may close their eyes or put their heads down on the desk if that helps them concentrate.

7. Before playing the song for the first time, ask students to think of a color that matches the emotion they feel while the song is playing. Play the song for the first time. When it ends, give students a moment to write down their color(s). Ask for volunteers to share their responses.

8. Before playing the song for the second time, ask students to think of a good title for the song. Play the song once more. When it ends, give students a moment to write down their title. Ask for volunteers to share their responses.

9. Reveal the actual title of the song. When do we send postcards? Why? Ask students to give an example of a message they might write in a postcard. We generally provide an update about ourselves and tell the addressee they are missed.

10. Before playing the song one last time, ask students to think of someone they love who is far away. Perhaps their best friend moved, or their cousin lives in another country, or their grandmother passed away. As they listen to the song, ask them to recall a special memory of that person: what activities did you do together? How did that person make you feel? What would you say to them now? Did they teach you anything important?

11. Play the song for the last time. When it ends, give students time to write a postcard message to their loved one. Urge them to include as much detail as possible. I usually make up a sample message: "Dear Grandma, I remember the time you took me to Coney Island and we went on the roller coaster. I was afraid but you held my hand and we had so much fun. Afterward we got chili dogs and mint ice cream. We sat on the boardwalk and listened to the squawking seagulls as the breeze blew off the ocean."

12. Ask for volunteers to share their responses. Be aware that some students may become emotional as they write and/or share their memories.

13. You can add an art component to this activity by making sankofa postcards. Simply make 2-sided photocopies on cardstock with the heart-shaped adinkra symbol on one side and lines on the other. Students can decorate the front of the postcard and

write a short message on the back. I put a photograph of my big brother in the center of the heart and drew a winter scene around it since my memory was of sledding late at night. I don't have an address for my brother but I recycled a stamp from Nevis, which is where my brother was born.

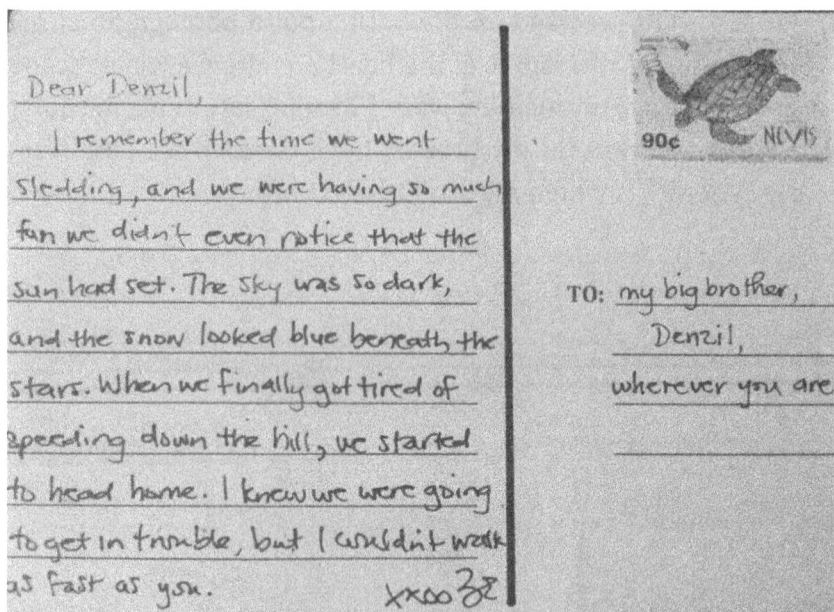

Dear Denzil,

I remember the time we went sledding, and we were having so much fun we didn't even notice that the sun had set. The sky was so dark, and the snow looked blue beneath the stars. When we finally got tired of speeding down the hill, we started to head home. I knew we were going to get in trouble, but I couldn't walk as fast as you.

xxoo

90¢    NEVIS

TO: my big brother,
        Denzil,
        wherever you are

## 2.

## Postcard to Poem

The second part of this workshop allows students to turn their postcards into poems.

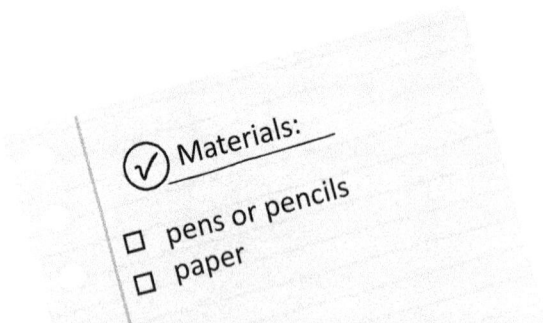

Materials:
☐ pens or pencils
☐ paper

1. I usually begin by sharing my completed postcard, which is addressed to my older brother Denzil. I give students a handout that shows my postcard message above my poem. Then I ask students to circle the words that appear in both.

Dear Denzil,

I remember the time we went sledding, and we were having so much fun we didn't even notice that the sun had set. The sky was so dark, and the snow looked blue beneath the stars. When we finally got tired of speeding down the hill, we started to head home. I knew we were going to be in trouble, but I couldn't walk as fast as you. My snowsuit was heavy and wet, and finally I just lay down in the street and cried up at the stars. You turned around, came back to where I lay in the middle of the road, and rolled me onto the sled. Then you pulled me the rest of the way home. I loved you more than ever that night, because you were my big brother, and you looked out for me.

XOXO Zetta

I remember the night sky dark as ink
blue shadows shifting beneath the pine trees
we flew downhill
giddy with speed
until it was time to go home
I was afraid
but you gave me courage
I was weak
but you gave me strength
your eyes that night were brighter than the stars
your skin like chocolate against the snow
wherever you are I hope you know
that I will always love you
brother

2. Once students are done circling the words, have them share their findings. Ask students to define the word "essence." I sometimes talk about how perfume is made or ask students which essential items they would grab if there was a fire in their home. Turning prose (their postcard message) into a poem requires students to extract the essence of their memory.

3. Ask students to review their postcard message and circle the 10 most important words.

4. Ask the students who have NOT previously shared their postcard messages to raise their hands. From these students, ask for volunteers to read their ten words aloud. Then ask if anyone in the class can piece together the memory using the hints or clues contained in the ten essential words. The volunteer can confirm or correct the narrative.

5. Ask students to consider the difference between poetry and prose. I use a handout to share examples and to provide some tools students can use when writing their free verse poems.

   **Your postcard was written in PROSE, but a poem is written in VERSE; PROSE is written in paragraphs, but poetry is written in stanzas. PROSE is written in complete sentences:**

   My grandmother took me to Coney Island.
   We ate cotton candy on the boardwalk.

**To turn PROSE into POETRY, we need to break those sentences into fragments:**

the summer sun
burning in the sky
salty sea breeze
wooden boards creaking
beneath our flip-flopped feet
sea gulls squawking
my hand held in yours
your smile sweet as
cotton candy

A **simile** compares two things using "like" or "as."

your smile sweet as / cotton candy

**Alliteration** is the repetition of an initial consonant sound.

salty sea
cotton candy
flip flop

6. To ensure that students understand what a simile is, ask them to complete these prompts:

| | |
|---|---|
| Sharp as... | a knife, a needle, a razor |
| Soft as... | a pillow, a cloud, a kitten |
| Quiet as... | a mouse, a library, an assassin |
| Hot like... | fire, the sun, lava, jalapeños |

7. Give students time to compose their poems. Ask for volunteers to share their poem with the class.

# 3.

## Postcard to Picture Book Story

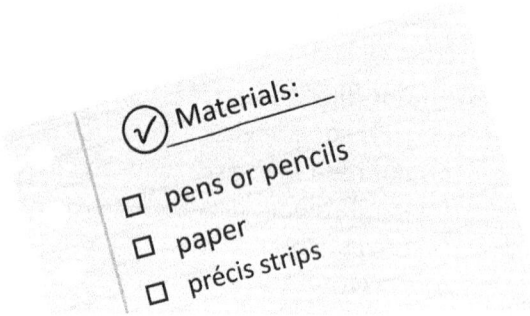

✓ Materials: _____

☐ pens or pencils

☐ paper

☐ précis strips

1. Warm up by having students work in groups to arrange the précis strips for BIRD.

2. Remind students that stories usually have a beginning, middle, and an end. When a story starts at A and ends at Z, we call that a LINEAR narrative. Action takes place sequentially. Bird is a NONLINEAR narrative because it starts at the end, after Marcus has already died, and then looks back at the events leading up to his death.

3. Illustrator Shadra Strickland used a symbol—Marcus' baseball cap—to signify absence. Ask students to think of an object that represents their person who's far away.

4. Ask students to consider the purpose of a blueprint. In order to build a strong story, writers need an outline. This is like the skeleton or bare bones of the story to which students will later "add flesh." Their story will need:

- A title: what words sum up your memory of this person?
- A setting: where does the action take place?
- A main character: YOU are the star of this story!
- A secondary character: this is the person who's far away (you can have more than one secondary character)
- A dilemma: can you think of a problem you once faced?
- A solution: how did your loved one help you solve your problem?
- A moral: did you learn a lesson from the person who helped you?
- A conclusion: not everyone lives "happily ever after," but your main character should show some sign of growth by the story's end

5. Ask students to write their story in TEN sentences. Remind them that they don't have to include a lot of details; those can be added later. For now, they just want to list the most important things that will happen to their characters.

1. _____

2. _____

3. _____

4. _____

5. _____

6. _____

7. _____

8. _____

9. _____

10. _____

I had a student whose memory involved learning to dive in the pool. His favorite aunt used to toss coins in the water, which encouraged him to move from the safety of the shallow end to the deep end of the pool. One day they spent the afternoon at the pool and his aunt lost her ring. The boy saw it at the bottom of the pool and found the courage to dive to the bottom of the deep end. Years later, his aunt moved away but she gave him the ring and he wore it around his neck on a chain. At the start of his story, the main character is fingering the ring around his neck and looking at a photograph taken at the neighborhood pool.

You can create a similar example to show students how you developed a story from one of your memories.

6. Once students have a basic outline for their story, they can expand each plot point. Ask students to consider how much text appears on the page of a picture book, and how it's arranged relative to the illustration. The art element of this activity involves students making pictures to accompany their story. See the Self-Publishing Resources chapter for tips on making picture books by hand.

# Melena's Jubilee

This activity was designed to accompany my picture book MELENA'S JUBILEE. I created three handouts with questions and space for students to write down their answers. Handouts can be hard to keep track of (I recommend giving students a writing folder in addition to a notebook), but I find they can also make writing seem more accessible—a handout with ten questions isn't as daunting to some students as a blank sheet of paper.

### Handout #1
### Your Ideal Day

Melena wakes up feeling like she's been given a second chance, so she does things differently throughout the day. Imagine that it's the first day of summer vacation. Answer the following questions to paint a picture of your ideal day.

1. What time would you wake up?

2. What would you eat for breakfast?

3. How would you spend the rest of the morning?

4. What would you eat for lunch?

5. How would you spend the afternoon?

6. What would you eat for dinner?

7. How would you spend the evening?

8. How much money would you need for your ideal day?

## Handout #2
# Your Fresh Start Day

Now that you've described your ideal day, let's change your routine so you can have your own jubilee!

1. Think of a conflict that might arise while you're doing your favorite activity:

2. Now think of a different way to resolve that conflict on your Fresh Start Day:

3. Think of your favorite meal. How could you make a meal for yourself or others without spending any money?

4. How could you help someone in your family or your neighborhood?

5. How might someone thank YOU for being generous and/or helpful?

## Handout #3

Write your story in TEN sentences! Don't include a lot of details; those can be added later. For now, you just want to list the most important things that will happen to your characters.

1. _____

2. _____

3. _____

4. _____

5. _____

6. _____

7. _____

8. _____

9. _____

10. _____

One student, José, shared that he enjoyed playing with Lego. For his Fresh Start Day, José said he would get up early and play with his active little brother so his mother could have a break. For dinner they would have his favorite food: pizza. I used elements of José's ideal day to develop responses for the second part of the activity.

1. Think of a conflict that might arise while you're doing your favorite activity:

   While José was building his Lego castle, his little brother Manny knocked it over and broke a special character given to him for his birthday. In an angry outburst, José slapped his little brother who started to cry loudly.

2. Now think of a different way to resolve that conflict on your Fresh Start Day:

   José knows Manny wants to play with him so he puts away his Lego set and takes his little brother to the park.

3. Think of your favorite meal. How could you make a meal for yourself or others without spending any money?

   See below.

4. How could you help someone in your family or your neighborhood?

José takes his little brother to the park and notices his elderly neighbor is cleaning up trash that is scattered all over her stoop. José asks Mrs. Rodriguez to watch his little brother while he cleans up the trash for her.

5. How might someone thank YOU for being generous and/or helpful?

Mrs. Rodriguez thanks José by giving him $10. Instead of buying a new Lego figurine, José buys a pizza and takes it home so his mother doesn't have to prepare a meal.

I read my responses out loud so students could see how I'd built a narrative around their classmate's ideal day. Then I shared my outline for the story, breaking it down into ten scenes.

1. José wakes up and hears his little brother crying—again.
2. José remembers slapping his brother the night before and feels bad.
3. José goes into the kitchen. His mother has a headache so he offers to take care of his brother for the day.
4. José pours his brother a bowl of cereal. Manny immediately knocks it onto the floor, making a mess.
5. José feels angry but doesn't get upset at Manny. Instead he makes toast for his brother and cleans up the mess.
6. José takes his brother to the park to play. They see their elderly neighbor cleaning up her stoop, which is littered with trash.
7. José offers to clean up if Mrs. Rodriguez watches Manny.
8. When the trash has been cleared, Mrs. Rodriguez thanks José by giving him $10!

9. José considers getting a new Lego figurine for himself but decides to buy a pizza instead.

10. José goes home and finds his mother feeling much better. She's glad she doesn't have to prepare a meal and they enjoy the delicious pizza.

Once students have finished their outline, they can begin writing and illustrating their picture book.

# What's Your Problem?

This writing workshop is designed to help students voice their opinion *and* consider alternate perspectives. You can draw upon any controversial issue—immigration, police violence, the impact of social media on teens. The questionnaire can be as detailed as you like; the handout I use has basic questions but could be modified to include gender, sexual orientation, religion, ability, ethnicity, class, etc. The effectiveness of the activity depends in large part upon the photo you select—try to find an engaging image that will inspire students to develop a profile that's significantly different than their own.

1.  Have students complete the questionnaire below.

    Name:

    Age:

    Favorite activity:

    Role model:

    Secret fear:

    Best quality or skill:

    Worst quality or skill:

    Dream job:

    Cause you care about most:

2.  Ask for volunteers to share their profile. Look for aspects of each student's identity that could lend itself to a dramatic narrative (a fear of being alone, memory trouble). Why are they invested in that particular cause?

3. Show students a picture of a diverse group of teens; this can be printed on a handout or displayed on a screen. Ask students to choose one teen, looking for visual cues (facial expression, clothing, pose/body language). Have students complete the same questionnaire to create a character for their script. Remind them that dramatic tension often comes from characters who have very different experiences, values, and points of view. To create a bond between two characters, one should have a strength that compensates for the other's weakness.

Name:

Age:

Favorite activity:

Role model:

Secret fear:

Best quality or skill:

Worst quality or skill:

Dream job:

Cause they care about most:

4. Ask for volunteers to share their profile. Why did they choose that particular person? Was it hard to develop an identity based solely on a photograph? Is this character someone the student would likely befriend?

5. Ask students to write a monologue that outlines their own point of view on a controversial topic like the student movement to end gun violence. Provide some guidance as they compose a short speech: can teens change public policy? Which matters more—mass shootings, police-involved shootings, or everyday

gun violence in low-income communities? Should guns be banned? Should teachers be armed?

6. Ask for volunteers to share their monologues.

7. Now ask students to write a monologue from the point of view of their character. How does their unique identity shape their particular point of view? Encourage students to consider variables that might shape their perspective on gun violence—what if the character's parent is a police officer? What if the character hunts recreationally? What if the character lost a sibling in a school shooting?

8. Ask for volunteers to share their character's monologue. Allow students to vote—which two characters would have the most dramatic dialogue? Which aspects of their identities are likely to produce tension?

9. At this point students can work in pairs or independently to write a dialogue—a short script—featuring two of their characters. How and why do their viewpoints differ? Can they find common ground and work together to find solutions to gun violence? If necessary, you can offer a provocative prompt to help students get started. For example, how would Character #2 respond if they heard this:

   Character #1: Hypocrite!

   This would likely cause Character #2 to feel defensive.

   Character #1: I can't get their blood off my hands.

   This would likely cause Character #2 to feel sympathetic or curious.

10. Once students have finished writing, give them time to rehearse their script before asking for volunteers to perform for the class. Ask students to reflect on the challenge of writing a character

with a different race, gender, background, or point of view. How do you humanize someone you may not like? How can a writer create sympathetic characters and avoid caricatures?

# A Wish after Midnight

When I present on my time-travel novel, I tell students how historic Weeksville was the second-largest free Black community in the US prior to the Civil War. I explain the causes of the Draft Riots of 1863 and show slides of the beautiful Brooklyn Botanic Garden where fifteen-year-old Genna Colon opens the portal that sends her back in time. The first writing activity focuses on contemporary issues of community and identity; the second activity asks students to imagine themselves playing a role in the riots. You can learn more about Weeksville at www.weeksvillesociety.org

## 1.

## You Don't Even Know Me

✓ Materials

☐ Chapter 10 of A WISH AFTER MIDNIGHT

☐ "You Don't Even Know Me" by Sharon Flake

☐ mirror handout

☐ pens

☐ magazines

☐ glue

☐ scissors

☐ construction paper

1. Have students warm up with a one-minute word association. Explain that they should write as quickly as possible BUT they may not name any person.

2. Set the timer and ask students to write down all the words they associate with "ghetto."

3. This is a difficult word so you may need to offer prompts: What does it mean to act ghetto? How do you know when you're in the ghetto? How do people dress? What do they eat? Where do they hang out?

4. When time's up, ask students whether it was challenging to come up with words. Then ask for volunteers to share their words, reminding them to scratch out any word that is provided by someone else.

5. Once all the words are on the board, note how many are positive. If all the words students shared are negative, ask them to consider words like "families," "block party," "neighbors," etc. Ask why those words didn't come to mind initially.

6. Ask students to consider the following ideas: Is "ghetto" a place or an attitude? Can you cross the street and know you've entered "the ghetto?" What does it mean to "act ghetto?" Can that kind of behavior ever give a person an advantage? What is the origin of the word "ghetto?" Are there any advantages to being part of a closed community? What are the disadvantages?

7. Distribute copies of, or ask students to turn to, Chapter 10 of AWAM. Give a brief recap so that students understand the characters they will encounter in this chapter of the novel. Read aloud together.

8. Ask students to reflect on Genna's encounter with Hannah. Why was Genna offended when Hannah offered to give her old clothes to Genna's mother? Does Hannah think Genna is "ghetto?" Why does Genna feel she has a tattoo on her forehead—how may that shape her future? What is the difference between wanting to SAVE someone and wanting to SERVE someone? What kind of help does Genna need to become independent?

9. Distribute copies of "You Don't Even Know Me." Ask students to profile the speaker and to note the shifting addressee as they read the poem (define addressee if necessary). Read aloud together.

10. Return to the beginning of the poem. Ask students to identify the speaker (a Black teenage boy). Ask students to name the four addressees: teacher, general public, neighbor, friend. What kind of nightmares might the speaker's father have about his son? "Only I define me"—is this true? Or do others define us? How do we "read" people?

11. Ask students to make two lists: how I see myself and how others see me. I usually make a handout with a mirror in the middle, which divides the page for the two columns of words. I share my own lists and then read aloud this poem, asking students to guess my addressee.

### "Read Me Right"

read me right
or don't read me at all
I walk down the street
and I hear you call
hey, princess!
light skin!
mami—hold up!

and when I don't stop
you spit ugly words
aimed like missiles
at my heart

think you're better than me?

I'm not better than anybody
and if you read me right
you'd know that I
earned
all I've got:
my PhD
the books that I wrote
the awards that I won
nothing was handed to me
on a silver platter
so I ignore all the chatter
the rumors and
the lies
if you read me right
you'd realize
that I'm pulling myself
up that ladder
one rung
at a
time

maybe I'll see you
at the
top

1. After 5-7 minutes, ask for volunteers to share their two lists. Then ask the volunteer to name one addressee—one person in their life who always reads them wrong. Where does the student encounter this person—in the hallway, on the bus, at home? Model the possible opening lines of their poem: "You see me at school/I may act the fool/but you don't see the lie/that hides behind my smile…"

2. Once students have shared their lists, they're ready to begin composing their poem. Remind them that there are no rules for free verse poetry—their poem doesn't have to rhyme, doesn't need punctuation, capitalization, etc. Remind them not to guess their addressee; there should be clues so that anyone reading the poem can identify the addressee.

3. Ask for volunteers to share their poems. Classmates can show their appreciation at the end by snapping (common practice at poetry readings). Ask students to guess the addressee in each poem.

4. You can add a visual element to this activity by having students make their own mirror. Provide magazines and/or ask students to bring in their favorite photos of themselves. These can be displayed inside of a gilt frame to reflect what students see when they look at themselves.

# 2.

## Meet Maritcha Lyons

Like my fictional character Genna Colon, Maritcha Lyons was a teenage witness to the horrors of the 1863 NYC Draft Riots. This workshop asks students to place themselves within a community rocked by racial tension and mob violence. Comparisons can be made to conditions in contemporary US.

(✓) Materials

☐ pens or pencils
☐ paper
☐ handouts
☐ Maritcha: a Nineteenth-Century American Girl by Tonya Bolden

1. Explain the word association warm-up activity; ask students to write the numbers one to ten down the margin of their sheet of paper.

2. Set the timer and give students one minute to write down as many words as they can that they associate with "riot." Younger students may respond better to a more familiar word—"war."

3. When time is up, ask students to put down their pens and share three of their words. If another student shares a word that's

on their list, it must be crossed off to avoid repetition. You can write students' words on the board to create a word cloud.

4. Ask students to consider the portrait of Maritcha Lyons on page 5 of *Maritcha: a Nineteenth-Century American Girl*. If a picture's worth a thousand words, what does this photograph say about this particular girl? Ask students to share what they know about the Underground Railroad, the Civil War, and the military draft. Have them consider how they might feel if they were caught in a riot today as Maritcha and her family were in 1863.

5. Read aloud Maritcha's first-hand account of the NYC Draft Riots (pages 33-43). Explain vocabulary words if 19th-century terms and/or objects are unclear. Ask students to make a list of the jobs held by the rioters. What role did the police play during the riot? How did neighbors help one another? What does the inventory compiled by Maritcha's father tell us about her status in society?

6. Distribute handout. CONTENT WARNING: offensive language.

## Handout #1

**Read the following monologue and look for clues to help you answer the questions at the end.**

I fixed him! I said I'd do it, and I did. Spent all morning on my knees, scrubbing Mrs. Williams' floors 'til they gleamed. By noon my poor back was aching so bad I could hardly stand. Cook offered me a cup of tea when the Missus wasn't looking—God bless her—and what do you think I saw out the very windows I'd scrubbed clean the day before? That high and mighty German loosening the nails in his backyard fence! I knew what he was about, though he couldn't see me watching him. Think they're so clever, these Germans—and they're sly, alright! Taking good jobs that any Irishman or woman could do just as well and for half the price. My poor Mikey's been doing odd jobs for months trying to help his poor Ma—and here come Germans like Scholz talking rot about the draft, saying it's the "moral duty" of every Christian man to take up arms and free the slaves. Free them to do what? I ask him. Come up here and take our jobs? And that German looked at me like I was something filthy from the gutter that he'd like to wipe off the sole of his shoe.

Well, I fixed him. Saw him loosening them boards and told my Mikey soon as I got home. Mikey and the boys broke into the boarding house the next day—you wouldn't believe all the fine things them niggers had in there! Every bit as nice as the things in Mrs. Williams' house that I dust and polish and can't ever hope to own myself. Well, the boys helped themselves to whatever they could lay their hands on. Mikey brought me a fine rug and a couple of fancy vases, though one of 'em got chipped in all the hustle and bustle.

Father McAvoy says it's a sin to covet and to steal. "Love they neighbor," he says. But why should I love them that don't love me? And what's the harm in taking a few trinkets the rich won't even miss? Scholz let the niggers pass through the fence and into his yard, and I hear they took the ferry over to Williamsburg. Plenty of German nigger-lovers out there! Good riddance, I say. They ought to put all of 'em on a boat and send 'em back to Africa where they belong! Mikey and the boys waited a couple of days and then caught Scholz on his way home from the pub—with a belly full of strong German ale, no doubt! Well, he won't treat the Irish like trash anymore, not without looking over his shoulder first. And I hear Scholz' son got called up for the draft. While he's laid up in bed licking his wounds he can think about all his fine ideas and whether freeing those God meant to be slaves is really worth his own son's life.

**Name:**

**Age:**

**Gender:**

**Race/Ethnicity:**

**Job:**

**Class:**

**How does this character feel about their neighbors? (African Americans, the Irish, Germans, the police)**

**What was their role in the riots?**

**How did this character's life change AFTER the riots?**

7. Give students time to write their own monologue using the above questions to develop their character's point of view. Ask for volunteers to share their work with the class. Students can then work in pairs to write a dialogue between community members impacted by the riots. You can use a provocative prompt such as, "I thought you were my friend!"

# Mythical Beasts

The activities that follow are from a creative writing "mini-camp" that I led for Uptown Stories in New York City. I have written several novels that feature mythical beasts: SHIP OF SOULS, THE PHOENIX ON BARKLEY STREET, THE PHANTOM UNICORN, and DRAGONS IN A BAG. Tales of strange and wonderful beasts—like mermaids, fairies, and trolls—exist in every culture. These creatures can be aggressive or elusive, dangerous or cuddly. They often need protection from a human friend, and in turn have abilities that can help humans achieve their goals. I was struck by the number of students in the mini-camp who incorporated social justice principles into their stories: a zombie wants to integrate his school, which keeps him segregated from humans; four magical creatures flee a prison camp and band together to stop the deforestation of their beloved home. The activities in this section are presented as handouts, though every day started with a warm-up and ended with in-class writing.

(✓) Materials

☐ handouts
☐ pens or pencils
☐ markers or colored pencils

1. Have students introduce themselves by giving their name and their favorite mythical beast.

2. Explain the word association warm-up activity; ask students to write the numbers one to ten down the margin of their sheet of paper.

3. Set the timer and give students one minute to write down as many words as they can that they associate with "monster."

4. When time is up, ask students to put down their pens and share three of their words. If another student shares a word that's on their list, it must be crossed off to avoid repetition. You can write students' words on the board to create a word cloud.

5. Ask students to consider whether they would have thought of different words if the prompt had been "mythical beasts" instead of "monsters." What's the difference? Why do we love some creatures and fear others? What can they teach us? What powers do they have that humans lack?

6. Ask students to create a profile for their creature; now have them DRAW their magical beast. Remind them that this could serve as the cover art for their book. We're told not to judge a book by its cover, but what makes a book appealing?

## Handout #1
# Creature Profile

Name & Species:
Age:
Place of origin. Was your creature born here or elsewhere?
Preferred home/habitat:
Favorite food:
Special abilities:
Weakness:
Enemy:
Ally:
Family:


The blank back of this handout can be used for students' illustration of their creature.

7.  Prepare students to write their first monologue by explaining the difference between first-, second-, and third-person point of view. I made a handout based on resources I found at *Grammerly.com*

## Handout #2
# Creature Monologue

Now that you've created a profile for your creature, write a MONOLOGUE. Answer the following questions from your creature's point of view:

1. What is it like to live on earth?
2. What do you think of humans?
3. How can your special powers help others?
4. How can humans help YOU?

_____

_____

_____

_____

_____

_____

_____

_____

_____

_____

_____

## Handout #3
# "Creating Complex Characters"

Complete the questionnaire below for YOURSELF.

Name:

Age:

Favorite activity:

Role model:

Secret fear:

Best quality or skill:

Worst quality or skill:

Dream job:

Mythical beast you like or fear most:


[insert photo of diverse kids]

Pick one child. Look for visual cues: facial expression, clothing, pose/body language. Now complete the questionnaire below to create a character for your story.

Name:

Age:

Favorite activity:

Role model:

Secret fear:

Best quality or skill:

Worst quality or skill:

Dream job:

Mythical beast they like or fear most:

## Handout #4
## Fiction Elements

1. TITLE: What word or phrase sums up your story?

_____

2. SETTING: Where does the action take place?

_____

3. MAIN CHARACTER: Who is the star of this story?

_____

4. ALLY: This is the person who will help your magical creature.

_____

5. ENEMY: This is the person trying to harm your creature.

_____

6. CHALLENGE: What problem must be solved?

_____

7. SOLUTION: How will your characters solve the problem?

_____

8. MORAL: Did your characters learn a lesson as they solved the problem? Your main character should show some sign of <u>growth</u> by the story's end.

_____

## Handout #5
## Dynamic Dialogue

Now imagine the first encounter between your creature and your human character. How will your creature reveal its special powers? How will they work together to overcome challenges?

HUMAN: Eeek! It's a _____.

CREATURE: Don't be afraid! I'm a _____.

HUMAN: _____.

CREATURE: _____.

HUMAN: _____.

CREATURE: _____.

HUMAN: _____.

CREATURE: _____.

HUMAN: _____.

CREATURE: _____.

HUMAN: _____.

CREATURE: _____.

## Handout #6
## Story Outline

Write your story in TEN sentences! Don't include a lot of details; those can be added later. For now, you just want to list the most important things that will happen to your characters. You can then develop each plot point into a chapter.

1. _____

2. _____

3. _____

4. _____

5. _____

6. _____

7. _____

8. _____

9. _____

10. _____

Write a three-sentence summary that will appear on the back cover of your book. What essential information will make kids want to read your book? Now write a one-sentence "pitch" that's sure to reel readers in!

## Handout #7
## The Value of a Villain

Are villains made or born? Can villains redeem themselves and become someone who helps rather than hurts? Write a monologue from the point of view of your villain. In "How I Became Bad," explain how your villain evolved over time. Which childhood experiences shaped them? Did your villain have a mentor—someone who taught them to be bad? Be sure to include a motive. What drives your villain—greed? Power? Revenge?

_____

_____

_____

_____

_____

_____

_____

_____

_____

_____

_____

# Peer Review

Peer review is an important part of the writing process. After reviewing the below critique tips, my students and I read aloud the first chapter of *Dragons in a Bag*.

- What information about my characters have I provided in this first chapter? What details have I left out? Why?

- Does this chapter "hook" you? Do you want to read more?

- How much description versus dialogue do I include?

Students then found a partner and shared a chapter of their story. As students review more of their peers' work, they can write promotional "blurbs" that can appear on the book cover.

## Handout #8
## Critique Tips

When you're <u>giving</u> feedback on a classmate's writing, keep the following in mind:

- **Put the author FIRST.** The critique is not for *you*—it's for the author. You're entitled to your own opinion but ask the author what to look for—pacing? Setting? Characterization? You're here to help.

- **Lead with what you like.** Be generous and praise the aspects you like FIRST so the author is encouraged to keep writing.

- **Be precise.** Try to be as specific as you can and avoid generalizations (like "It's good" or "This doesn't work for me"). Don't just share what you like or dislike, tell the author *why*.

- **Consider the audience**. Ask the author about their intended audience. (It may not be you!)

- **Take notes**. If you are listening to a story, you may not remember issues by the time it ends. Take notes as the author is reading, or write your thoughts down as you read a printed story.

- **Find solutions, not just problems**. Offer examples of ways to improve the areas that need more work.

When you're <u>receiving</u> feedback on your own writing, keep the following in mind:

- **Accept advice.** Understand that feedback can help you become a better writer.

- **Don't take it personally.** Everyone is entitled to their own opinion. Find what's useful in the critique and apply it to the story, not to yourself.

- **Take notes.** Listen carefully as your receive feedback and write it all down—even if you disagree. Later you can pick out the most useful advice.

- **Don't get defensive.** You are *not* under attack! Trust that the feedback is intended to make you a better writer—not to hurt your feelings.

- **Keep writing!** It's nice to please your audience but it's important to please yourself, too! Keep working on a story until <u>you</u> are satisfied. Remember that you grow as a writer by taking risks and making mistakes.

## Handout #9
# People & Places

Fantasy fiction requires you to build a world where anything is possible. To make your characters and scenes intriguing, it's important to give readers interesting descriptions of the people and places in your story. If you had to describe yourself to a stranger, which *distinguishing features* would you include? (things that make you stand out in a crowd) I would tell the person that I have curly brown hair, purple glasses, and I almost always have a book in my hand.

Describe yourself:                              _____

 

                                                               _____

 

                                                               _____

Describe this room:                            _____

 

                                                               _____

 

                                                               _____

Describe your protagonist:                 _____

 

                                                               _____

 

                                                               _____

Describe your creature:

_____

_____

_____

Describe their habitat:

_____

_____

_____

Describe your villain:

_____

_____

_____

## Handout #10
# Writing a Meaningful Conclusion

Answer the following questions and think about what YOU want readers to take away from your story.

1.  When I finish reading a story, I like to feel:

    a) satisfied     b) curious     c) confused     d) happy

    e) breathless     f) teary

2.  A story must have a happy ending:     T     F

3.  Characters should be better people by the end of a story:

    T   F

4.  All problems must be solved by the end of a story:
    T   F

5.  Pick one word to describe how you want your reader to feel at the end of your story:

6.  Every hero has at least one flaw. What is your main character's flaw or weakness?

7.  How does your main character change or grow by the end of your story?

8.  What's the takeaway? Has your story taught the reader anything about life and/or human nature?

# Self-Publishing Resources

When your students have completed their stories, they can publish their own books using print-on-demand (POD) technology, which is affordable and fast. I have self-published over twenty books using CreateSpace, a POD site owned by Amazon. I've also used Lulu, and Ingram Spark is another option.

I have also used POD platforms to publish student work. Using interior and cover templates that can be downloaded for free, it's easy to assemble an anthology of student writing, artwork, and/or photography. Self-published books can be sold online or at school events; they can be used to raise funds or to celebrate a milestone like graduation. These are some student anthologies I made using templates:

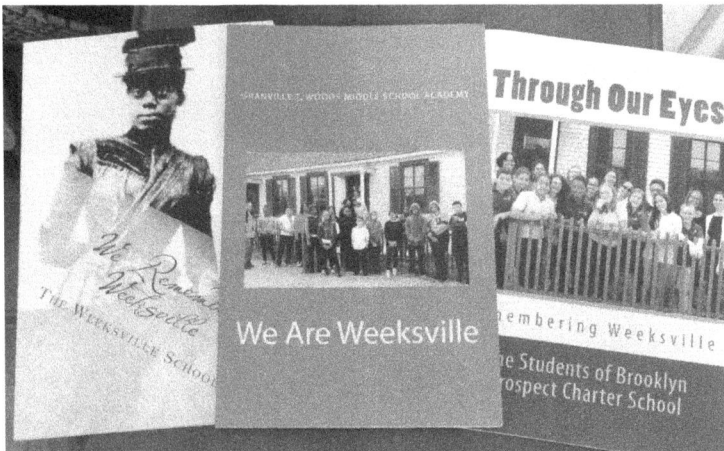

Maya Gonzalez has developed a fantastic site for student writers:

www.writenowmakebooks.com

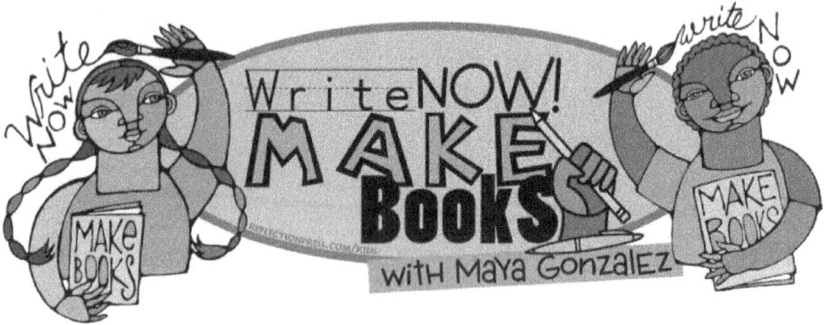

She also has additional resources on the Reflection Press website:

http://www.reflectionpress.com/free-stuff/we-the-people-self-publishing-resources/

# ABOUT THE AUTHOR

Born in Canada, Zetta Elliott moved to the US in 1994 to pursue her PhD in American Studies at NYU. Her poetry has been published in several anthologies, and her plays have been staged in New York and Chicago. Her essays have appeared in *The Huffington Post*, *School Library Journal*, and *Publishers Weekly*. She is the author of thirty books for young readers, including the award-winning picture book *Bird*. Her urban fantasy novel, *Ship of Souls*, was named a *Booklist* Top Ten Sci-fi/Fantasy Title for Youth; her YA novel, *The Door at the Crossroads,* was a finalist in the Speculative Fiction category of the 2017 Cybils Awards and her picture book, *Melena's Jubilee*, won a 2017 Skipping Stone Award. Three books published under her own imprint, Rosetta Press, have been named Best Children's Books of the Year by the Bank Street Center for Children's Literature. Rosetta Press generates culturally relevant stories that center children who have been marginalized, misrepresented, and/or rendered invisible in traditional children's literature. Elliott is an advocate for greater diversity and equity in publishing. She currently lives in Philadelphia. Learn more at www.zettaelliott.com.

Printed in the USA
CPSIA information can be obtained
at www.ICGtesting.com
LVHW090028231023
761811LV00004BA/489

9 781987 455656